Everything You Ever Wanted to Know About...

Everything You Ever Wanted to Know About......

Absolutely nothing, because we really don't care...

Everything You Ever Wanted to Know About...

Absolutely nothing, because we really don't care...

Everything You Ever Wanted to Know About...

Absolutely nothing, because we really don't care...

Everything You Ever Wanted to Know About...

Absolutely nothing, because we really don't care...

Everything You Ever Wanted to Know About...

Absolutely nothing, because we really don't care...

Everything You Ever Wanted to Know About...

Absolutely nothing, because we really don't care...

Everything You Ever Wanted to Know About...

Absolutely nothing, because we really don't care...

Everything You Ever Wanted to Know About...

Absolutely nothing, because we really don't care...

Everything You Ever Wanted to Know About…

Absolutely nothing, because we really don't care…

Everything You Ever Wanted to Know About...

Absolutely nothing, because we really don't care...

Everything You Ever Wanted to Know About...

Absolutely nothing, because we really don't care...

12

Everything You Ever Wanted to Know About...

Absolutely nothing, because we really don't care....

Everything You Ever Wanted to Know About....

Absolutely nothing, because we really don't care...

Everything You Ever Wanted to Know About...

Absolutely nothing, because we really don't care…..

Everything You Ever Wanted to Know About…..

Absolutely nothing, because we really don't care…

Everything You Ever Wanted to Know About...

Absolutely nothing, because we really don't care...

Everything You Ever Wanted to Know About...

Absolutely nothing, because we really don't care...

———

Everything You Ever Wanted to Know About...

Absolutely nothing, because we really don't care...

Everything You Ever Wanted to Know About...

Absolutely nothing, because we really don't care...

Everything You Ever Wanted to Know About...

Absolutely nothing, because we really don't care...

Everything You Ever Wanted to Know About...

Absolutely nothing, because we really don't care...

Everything You Ever Wanted to Know About...

Absolutely nothing, because we really don't care...

Everything You Ever Wanted to Know About...

Absolutely nothing, because we really don't care...

Everything You Ever Wanted to Know About...

Absolutely nothing, because we really don't care...

Everything You Ever Wanted to Know About...

Absolutely nothing, because we really don't care...

Everything You Ever Wanted to Know About...

Absolutely nothing, because we really don't care...

Everything You Ever Wanted to Know About...

Absolutely nothing, because we really don't care...

Everything You Ever Wanted to Know About...

Absolutely nothing, because we really don't care...

Everything You Ever Wanted to Know About...

Absolutely nothing, because we really don't care...

Everything You Ever Wanted to Know About...

Absolutely nothing, because we really don't care...

Everything You Ever Wanted to Know About...

Absolutely nothing, because we really don't care...

Everything You Ever Wanted to Know About...

Absolutely nothing, because we really don't care...

Everything You Ever Wanted to Know About...

Absolutely nothing, because we really don't care...

Everything You Ever Wanted to Know About...

Absolutely nothing, because we really don't care....

Everything You Ever Wanted to Know About….

Absolutely nothing, because we really don't care…

Everything You Ever Wanted to Know About...

Absolutely nothing, because we really don't care...

Everything You Ever Wanted to Know About...

Absolutely nothing, because we really don't care...

Everything You Ever Wanted to Know About...

Absolutely nothing, because we really don't care...

Everything You Ever Wanted to Know About...

Absolutely nothing, because we really don't care...

Everything You Ever Wanted to Know About....

Absolutely nothing, because we really don't care...

Everything You Ever Wanted to Know About....

Absolutely nothing, because we really don't care...

Everything You Ever Wanted to Know About...

Absolutely nothing, because we really don't care...

Everything You Ever Wanted to Know About...

Absolutely nothing, because we really don't care...

Everything You Ever Wanted to Know About...

Absolutely nothing, because we really don't care...

Everything You Ever Wanted to Know About...

Absolutely nothing, because we really don't care...

Everything You Ever Wanted to Know About...

Absolutely nothing, because we really don't care.....

Everything You Ever Wanted to Know About…..

Absolutely nothing, because we really don't care…

Everything You Ever Wanted to Know About...

Absolutely nothing, because we really don't care...

Everything You Ever Wanted to Know About...

Absolutely nothing, because we really don't care...

Everything You Ever Wanted to Know About...

Absolutely nothing, because we really don't care...

Everything You Ever Wanted to Know About...

Absolutely nothing, because we really don't care...

Everything You Ever Wanted to Know About...

Absolutely nothing, because we really don't care...

Everything You Ever Wanted to Know About...

Absolutely nothing, because we really don't care...

Everything You Ever Wanted to Know About...

Absolutely nothing, because we really don't care...

Everything You Ever Wanted to Know About...

Absolutely nothing, because we really don't care...

Everything You Ever Wanted to Know About...

Absolutely nothing, because we really don't care...

Everything You Ever Wanted to Know About...

Absolutely nothing, because we really don't care...

Everything You Ever Wanted to Know About...

Absolutely nothing, because we really don't care....

Everything You Ever Wanted to Know About…..

Absolutely nothing, because we really don't care…

Everything You Ever Wanted to Know About...

Absolutely nothing, because we really don't care...

Everything You Ever Wanted to Know About...

Absolutely nothing, because we really don't care….

Everything You Ever Wanted to Know About...

Absolutely nothing, because we really don't care...

Everything You Ever Wanted to Know About...

Absolutely nothing, because we really don't care...

Everything You Ever Wanted to Know About...

Absolutely nothing, because we really don't care...

Everything You Ever Wanted to Know About...

Absolutely nothing, because we really don't care...

Everything You Ever Wanted to Know About...

Absolutely nothing, because we really don't care....

Everything You Ever Wanted to Know About….

Absolutely nothing, because we really don't care…

Everything You Ever Wanted to Know About...

Absolutely nothing, because we really don't care...

Everything You Ever Wanted to Know About...

Absolutely nothing, because we really don't care...

Everything You Ever Wanted to Know About...

Absolutely nothing, because we really don't care...

Everything You Ever Wanted to Know About...

Absolutely nothing, because we really don't care...

Everything You Ever Wanted to Know About...

Absolutely nothing, because we really don't care...

Everything You Ever Wanted to Know About...

Absolutely nothing, because we really don't care...

Everything You Ever Wanted to Know About...

Absolutely nothing, because we really don't care...

Everything You Ever Wanted to Know About...

Absolutely nothing, because we really don't care......

Everything You Ever Wanted to Know About...

Absolutely nothing, because we really don't care...

Everything You Ever Wanted to Know About...

Absolutely nothing, because we really don't care...

Everything You Ever Wanted to Know About...

Absolutely nothing, because we really don't care....

Everything You Ever Wanted to Know About...

Absolutely nothing, because we really don't care...

Everything You Ever Wanted to Know About...

Absolutely nothing, because we really don't care...

Everything You Ever Wanted to Know About...

Absolutely nothing, because we really don't care...

___

Everything You Ever Wanted to Know About...

Absolutely nothing, because we really don't care...

———

Everything You Ever Wanted to Know About...

Absolutely nothing, because we really don't care...

Everything You Ever Wanted to Know About...

Absolutely nothing, because we really don't care...

Everything You Ever Wanted to Know About...

Absolutely nothing, because we really don't care...

Everything You Ever Wanted to Know About...

Absolutely nothing, because we really don't care...

Everything You Ever Wanted to Know About...

Absolutely nothing, because we really don't care...

Everything You Ever Wanted to Know About...

Absolutely nothing, because we really don't care...

———

Everything You Ever Wanted to Know About...

Absolutely nothing, because we really don't care...

Everything You Ever Wanted to Know About...

Absolutely nothing, because we really don't care....

Everything You Ever Wanted to Know About....

Absolutely nothing, because we really don't care...

Everything You Ever Wanted to Know About...

Absolutely nothing, because we really don't care...

Everything You Ever Wanted to Know About...

Absolutely nothing, because we really don't care...

Everything You Ever Wanted to Know About...

Absolutely nothing, because we really don't care...

Everything You Ever Wanted to Know About...

Absolutely nothing, because we really don't care...

Everything You Ever Wanted to Know About...

Absolutely nothing, because we really don't care...

Everything You Ever Wanted to Know About...

Absolutely nothing, because we really don't care...

Everything You Ever Wanted to Know About...

Absolutely nothing, because we really don't care...

Everything You Ever Wanted to Know About...

Absolutely nothing, because we really don't care...

Everything You Ever Wanted to Know About...

Absolutely nothing, because we really don't care...

Everything You Ever Wanted to Know About...

Absolutely nothing, because we really don't care...

Everything You Ever Wanted to Know About...

.

Absolutely nothing, because we really don't care...

Everything You Ever Wanted to Know About...

Absolutely nothing, because we really don't care...

Everything You Ever Wanted to Know About...

Absolutely nothing, because we really don't care...

Everything You Ever Wanted to Know About...

Absolutely nothing, because we really don't care...

Everything You Ever Wanted to Know About...

Absolutely nothing, because we really don't care...

———

Everything You Ever Wanted to Know About...

Absolutely nothing, because we really don't care...

Everything You Ever Wanted to Know About...

Absolutely nothing, because we really don't care...

Everything You Ever Wanted to Know About...

Absolutely nothing, because we really don't care...

Everything You Ever Wanted to Know About...

Absolutely nothing, because we really don't care...

Everything You Ever Wanted to Know About...

Absolutely nothing, because we really don't care...

Everything You Ever Wanted to Know About...

Absolutely nothing, because we really don't care...

Everything You Ever Wanted to Know About...

Absolutely nothing, because we really don't care...

Everything You Ever Wanted to Know About...

Absolutely nothing, because we really don't care...

Everything You Ever Wanted to Know About...

Absolutely nothing, because we really don't care...

Everything You Ever Wanted to Know About...

Absolutely nothing, because we really don't care...

Everything You Ever Wanted to Know About...

Absolutely nothing, because we really don't care...

Everything You Ever Wanted to Know About...

Absolutely nothing, because we really don't care...

Everything You Ever Wanted to Know About...

Absolutely nothing, because we really don't care...

Everything You Ever Wanted to Know About....

Absolutely nothing, because we really don't care...

Everything You Ever Wanted to Know About...

Absolutely nothing, because we really don't care…..

Everything You Ever Wanted to Know About...

Absolutely nothing, because we really don't care...

Everything You Ever Wanted to Know About...

Absolutely nothing, because we really don't care...

Everything You Ever Wanted to Know About...

Absolutely nothing, because we really don't care...

Everything You Ever Wanted to Know About...

Absolutely nothing, because we really don't care...

Everything You Ever Wanted to Know About...

Absolutely nothing, because we really don't care...

Everything You Ever Wanted to Know About...

Absolutely nothing, because we really don't care...

Everything You Ever Wanted to Know About...

Absolutely nothing, because we really don't care...

Everything You Ever Wanted to Know About...

Absolutely nothing, because we really don't care...

Absolutely nothing at all, because we really don't care...

10247128R00077

Printed in Germany
by Amazon Distribution
GmbH, Leipzig